T0268087

Haven

Also by Mishka Lavigne

from Éditions l'Interligne
Cinéma (2016)
Havre (2018)
Copeaux (2020)

from Playwrights Canada Press
Shorelines (2023)

Haven

Mishka Lavigne

translated by Neil Blackadder

Playwrights Canada Press
Toronto

For professional or amateur production rights, please contact:
Catherine Mensour, Mensour Agency
kate@mensour.ca | 613.241.1677

LIBRARY AND ARCHIVES CANADA CATALOGUING IN PUBLICATION
Title: Haven / Mishka Lavigne ; translated by Neil Blackadder.
Other titles: Havre. English
Names: Lavigne, Mishka, 1984- author. | Blackadder, Neil Martin, 1963- translator.
Description: First English edition. | A play. | Translation of: Havre.
Identifiers: Canadiana (print) 20230168353 | Canadiana (ebook) 20230168450
  | ISBN 9780369104250 (softcover) | ISBN 9780369104267 (PDF)
  | ISBN 9780369104274 (EPUB)
Classification: LCC PS8623.A835355 H3813 2023 | DDC C842/.6—dc23

Playwrights Canada Press operates on land which is the ancestral home of the Anishinaabe Nations (Ojibwe / Chippewa, Odawa, Potawatomi, Algonquin, Saulteaux, Nipissing, and Mississauga), the Wendat, and the members of the Haudenosaunee Confederacy (Mohawk, Oneida, Onondaga, Cayuga, Seneca, and Tuscarora), as well as Metis and Inuit peoples. It always was and always will be Indigenous land.

We acknowledge the financial support of the Canada Council for the Arts, the Ontario Arts Council (OAC), Ontario Creates, and the Government of Canada for our publishing activities.

Canada Council
for the Arts

Conseil des arts
du Canada

ONTARIO ARTS COUNCIL
CONSEIL DES ARTS DE L'ONTARIO
an Ontario government agency
un organisme du gouvernement de l'Ontario

ONTARIO | ONTARIO
CREATES | CRÉATIF

Havre was first produced in French by La
Troupe du Jour, Saskatoon, from September 26
to October 4, 2018, with the following cast and
creative team:

Elsie: Alicia Johnston
Matt: Paul Fruteau De Laclos

Director: David Granger
Assistant Director: Anique Granger
Sound Design: Gilles Zolty
Set Design: Teagan O'Bertos
Costume Design: Denis Rouleau
Stage Manager: Jesse Fulcher Gagnon
Technical Director: Frank Engel
English Surtitles: Shavaun Liss from the transla-
tion by Neil Blackadder

The play was first produced in English as *Haven* in a staged reading at the International Voices Project, Chicago, on May 22, 2018. It was translated by Neil Blackadder and directed by Anna Bahow.

Further edits were made following Zoom readings in preparation for the play's first full production by United Players of Vancouver at the Jericho Arts Centre from January 28 to February 3, 2022. The production featured the following cast and creative team:

Elsie: Tina Georgieva
Matt: Alexander Lowe

Director: Jack Paterson
Assistant Director: Hannah Siden
Technical Director: Karen Chiang
Lighting Design: Vanka Chaitra Salim
Set and Projection Design: Joel Grinke
Costume Design: Shasta Lily Barkman
Sound Design: Georgia Couver
Stage Manager: Maria Denholme

Characters

Elsie
Matt

Prologue

A deep intake of breath.

ELSIE

MATT
June 14.

ELSIE
At 5:21 a.m.
Eastern Daylight Time.

MATT
At 11:21 a.m.
British Summer Time.

ELSIE
Ottawa.
Sandy Hill.

MATT
London.
Heathrow Airport.

ELSIE
A massive noise
like an explosion.

It's enough to wake the dead.

On June 14, at the end of a cul-de-sac, an enormous hole tears open the asphalt, and a car that was parked in the street falls into the hole, straight down towards the bottom. A red car.

MATT
On June 14, a man waits at Gate 42, holding a cup of coffee and his passport. He's been travelling all night. He's dead tired.

ELSIE
The red car that crashed into the hole at 5:21 had nobody in it. Just an old

ELSIE
MATT
coffee-stained

ELSIE
copy of the novel *Haven* by Gabrielle Sauriol.

MATT
11:21 a.m.
Takeoff.

ELSIE
5:21 a.m.
Neighbours come out of their houses
hurry to the edge of the chasm.

Someone calls 911.

MATT

The plane climbs up to where the sun's shining.
The plane glides west.
The man gets back the hours he's already lived
one by one the hours are sucked into the plane's engines
then spat back out
on the other side.

"Ladies and gentlemen, the captain has turned on the seat-belt sign in
anticipation of an area of turbulence. Kindly comply by returning to
your seats."

He closes his eyes
tries to sleep
but the plane rocks from side to side
he feels nausea rising.

ELSIE

One of the neighbours, cellphone in hand,
explains the situation to the 911 dispatcher:
a hole in the pavement
a car at the bottom of the hole
nobody in the car, it looks like.
With one hand, he's holding his phone
with the other he's gesticulating
as if the person at the other end could see him.

A woman stands on the lawn under her balcony
tired, confused, woken up with a start.

MATT
The plane shakes
the floor vibrates
the passengers hold their breath.

"The captain has turned on the seat-belt sign. The captain has the situation well in hand. The captain is in control. The captain is here for you now. The captain is your saviour. The captain holds the key to life and death and everything."

Look straight ahead.
Feeling nauseous.
From one moment to the next, the plane stops getting tossed around
all the passengers breathe again.
Including him.

ELSIE
The woman walks up to the hole to have a look at the red car.
The neighbour talking on the phone holds her back by the arm.
"Watch out!" he tells her. "It's dangerous."
She apologizes
but he's not listening to her
he nods, with the phone stuck to his ear.

MATT
The man's returning from Sarajevo.
He's flying west.

The last flight before he gets back home.
The man tears up, one after another, the boarding passes from his previous flights.

Sarajevo–Vienna
Vienna–London
London–Ottawa

The flight attendant comes past with a trash bag.
The man takes all the pieces of paper
and drops them in the bag that's being held out to him
and he doesn't feel a thing
just an enormous emptiness and enormous fatigue.

"Ladies and gentlemen, we are beginning our descent into
Macdonald–Cartier International Airport. Local time in Ottawa is
11:55 a.m. with a beautiful sunny twenty-three degrees Celsius. Thank
you for choosing to fly with us today."

Landing in Ottawa.
Hours that feel like lifetimes.
The baggage carousel turns.
The man looks around as he waits.
On all the TV screens in the terminal
the screens that broadcast news in a loop with no sound
in all the subtitles running along the bottom
the man sees the same name again and again:
"Gabrielle Sauriol."

ELSIE
The neighbour on his cellphone is still gesticulating.
Suddenly a police car shows up
then another one.
The police move the curious people away from the hole
people talk
the lights turn
blue red blue.

MATT
He sees the name that's being repeated on all the screens
one TV in French
one TV in English
"Gabrielle Sauriol"
but it doesn't really mean anything to him
so he doesn't take it in
he doesn't take anything in.

ELSIE
The woman's cellphone rings.
The screen displays an area code for British Columbia
and the letters "RCMP."

She answers:
Yes. This is she.
Yes. She's my mother.
Why?

ELSIE
MATT
On June 14 at 2:21 a.m. Pacific Daylight Time, the car being driven by
the writer Gabrielle Sauriol went off Island Highway at high speed and
crashed into a tree. Gabrielle Sauriol was ejected through the wind-
shield of her car into the Pacific Ocean around the level of Discovery
Passage. The Canadian coast guard and the emergency services are still
looking for the writer's body.

ELSIE
It's 6:04 a.m.
Time comes to a stop.
Everything collapses and another chasm opens up.

The earth swallows her.
Her world crumbles.

A deep intake of breath. An exhalation. Then silence.

One

ELSIE

Day three. Funeral home.

I'm in mourning.

That's what one says, right?

That's what one says.

MATT

I went to Sarajevo, in Bosnia–Herzegovina,

the city where I'm told I was born.

I wanted everything to look familiar

I wanted something to get triggered

I wanted all my childhood memories to come rushing back to me

but I didn't recognize a thing.

I don't remember anything.

ELSIE

My sincere condolences.

Thank you.

My most sincere condolences.

Thank you.

All my sympathy.

Thank you.

Condooooolences.

Thank youuuuu.

Sincere . . .

Tha . . .

MATT

If I can't remember my memories anymore
are they still memories?
Should we maybe say
forgettings instead?

ELSIE

I shake hands because it's what one does.
I shake hand after hand
so many that I start wondering which one is mine.

MATT

Even after all these years, nothing's been repaired.
Not really.
They want everyone to see
everyone to know
that there was a war here.
Sarajevo and its ghosts.

ELSIE

Here lies Gabrielle Sauriol—not . . .
not really
Gabrielle Sauriol lies in the Pacific Ocean now.

MATT

Another place had welcomed me
given me a family
an ideal family
a couple who'd been waiting for a child for so long
that a nine-year-old child shattered by war
a nine-year-old whose whole past had been wiped out
was better than no child at all.

ELSIE
I'm in mourning.
I'm wearing black.
I shake people's hands.
I say thank you
because I'm polite.
I'm well-brought-up.
The well-brought-up daughter of Gabrielle Sauriol.

MATT
I looked for the address that showed up in my file
in that pile of papers that
according to them
is me.
That according to them is the only trace of my existence.

With my interpreter Sanel
I looked for the orphanage where I spent one and a half years of my life
and I never found it.

Number sixteen—now it's a bank.

"I'm sorry, my friend," Sanel said to me in English.

I was looking for answers
and I didn't even find any questions.

Whole pieces of my life are missing
nine years
a whole city
a whole continent
my parents' faces are missing.

ELSIE

My friends call me, text me, email me.
They want to know how I'm doing.
"Do you need us, Elsie?
We're here for you for everything you need let us know what you'd like
we understand it's difficult but don't hesitate Elsie we're going to help
you as best we can write me call me don't stay on your own."
First one message
then two, a dozen, then thirty.
"Elsie, call me back."
Too many messages.
I don't reply to anyone.
My cellphone's been in a drawer since yesterday.

MATT

In Sarajevo, people talk to me in a language I no longer understand
a language I deleted at the same time as everything else.
I wanted to patch together the pieces of my life from before.
I'd have liked it if people had said to me
we've been expecting you
we couldn't wait for you to come back.
I'd have liked to recoup my life
to understand
but I didn't find anything over there
so I retraced my steps
westwards:
Sarajevo
Vienna
London
and further west still.
Ottawa.

ELSIE

People tell me:

You need to take the time to come to terms with this.

"Come to terms with it"

as if this was a legal dispute.

A piece of me is missing.

Two

ELSIE
My mother
er
I'm sorry.

We've gathered here today to pay our respects to my mother.

"There are some moments that are beyond us."
That's the first sentence on the first page of *Haven*.
But you knew that.
Everybody knows that.

This here, now: this is a moment that's beyond us.

We all know that the writing of Gabrielle Sauriol speaks better
than I do.

We all know you're here for her
and that I
I'm here for a Gabrielle Sauriol you don't know.

MATT
Sitting on the old brown sofa
the old sofa that used to be in my parents' house
I look outside.

My earliest memory:
I'm nine years old and I'm sitting on this brown sofa.
On the wall opposite the sofa
a deer head.
I'd never seen one of those before:
a deer head.

without the body
just a head

ELSIE
That's not my mother
the Governor General's Award, the Femina, the Booker, and all the others
the honorary doctorates
the millions of Twitter followers
the articles in all the magazines
the appointments as writer-in-residence
that's not my mother.
My mother is someone else.

MATT
The glass eyes of the deer look at me
as if they can see through me.

I really need to go to the bathroom.
I walk as far as the kitchen
and there they are
talking about me.

Him and her: a couple.
And her: an older woman surrounded by piles of papers.

She's the person who brought me here in a white car.

I use my hands to signal that I need the bathroom.
They understand and the man shows me the way.
I see he wants to put his hand on my shoulder
but changes his mind
so as not to frighten me
as if I was a wounded animal.

ELSIE
I never knew my father.
It's always just been her and me.
No other family besides her.
My mother
was the one who read with me late into the evening
pressed right up together in my little bed.
She was the one who knew how to light a fire in five minutes flat
those times we got on the road to go to seedy campgrounds
on Prince Something or Other Island
in the Whatever Valley
by the River I Forget What It Was Called.
She was the one who cried
every time she heard Neil Young's "Helpless."
She was the one I clung on to as tightly as I could
when I swam in the Pacific for the first time.

MATT
In the bathroom, I look around:
wallpaper with birds on it
a pink shell decorating the edge of the bathtub
towels so white and so soft.
And above the toilet

a tiny window that you open by sliding the glass panels.
I think about the deer's eyes
about the people in the kitchen
about the language they're speaking that I can't understand
then I'm standing on the toilet
and then I'm outside in the snow
in my stocking feet.
To my right, a fence and a swimming pool
to my left, a narrow gravel path that leads to the street.

In the street
my hair wet from the snow
my socks soon soaking wet
my sweater covered in snowflakes.

Unable to read the signs and the posters
unable to understand anything in this place
except the snow.

I walk.
I get to the end of the street.
Right, left.
It looks just the same and unfamiliar in both directions.

Standing there in the falling snow
I hear someone shouting.

They're running towards me
she holding a blanket
he with big boots on his feet.
The man puts his arms round me
hoists me up off the ground and wraps me up in the blanket
then they take me back to the house with the dead deer.

For weeks, stuck on the refrigerator with magnets
a smudged printout, slightly torn in one corner
with my name
and the names of the man with the boots
and the woman with the blanket.

They never asked me to call them Mom and Dad
but I did anyway
and the first time
they cried.

ELSIE
My mother isn't here.
But you know that.
Everybody knows that her remains aren't here today.
She's decomposing
she's sinking
she's being shaken up by the tide
eaten up by the deep-sea creatures.

Beat.

That's macabre.
I'm sorry.
That's not what you came here for.
You have to read *Haven* to understand grief.
In *Haven*
a mother loses her daughter
and I've . . .
It's the same
it's nearly the same.

In the novel, the mother gets to see the daughter's body
touch it
in order to really understand that she's no longer living in that body.
In the novel, they bring her daughter's body back to her
they prove to her that her daughter's gone.

I sound like I'm in my classroom.
I'm sorry.
That's not what you came here for.

Beat.

Thank you for coming to honour the memory of my mother. For information about any posthumous tributes you'd like to pay to her, please contact Mr. O'Neill, the lawyer for the publishing house.

Have a good rest of your day.

Three

ELSIE
I try to dissolve into the decor of the funeral home.
All around me
my mother's admirers are drinking coffee
eating hors d'oeuvres
exchanging business cards
as if this was a normal day and a normal place.
They keep looking in my direction
and I can hear they're talking about me in hushed tones
about what I said earlier in front of everyone.
When they see that I'm looking at them, they nod at me
and then return to their business, their ideas, their finger food.
And further away, my friends.
They dressed in black, they're talking among themselves.
They're wondering which of them I called over the last few days.
Philippe looks at Julia who looks at François who looks at Ravi who
looks at Katherine and they all look at Geneviève
who
looks
at me.

I didn't return their calls
not one of them.

Geneviève moves away from the group and comes towards me.
She's teetering in her high heels on the deep-pile carpet.
Once she's reached me, she leans towards my ear.
"Elsie . . . what can I do? Tell me what I can do. Do you want to leave? I
can take you home. Leave them to it, the rest of them. We can take you
home if that's what you want. Tell me how we can help you."

I don't answer.
I have a lump in my throat.
Geneviève holds my hand in hers
something she never does
holding my hand.

MATT
There's a knock and there she is
at the door of what
not so long ago
was our apartment.

She's coming back from yoga, wearing her red headband, her bag over
her shoulder.
"My mail, Matt?"
she says, without a smile, as she reaches out her hand.

Is that new? Your watch?
I ask her.
Not even a fraction of a second of silence.
"I bought myself a watch. Is that allowed?"

I don't answer. I give her the pile of envelopes with her name on them.
Her name and our address.
No, that's wrong.
Her name and my address.

She goes away without saying anything else.
I watch her leave
like it's a film.

ELSIE
I'm sitting in the restroom of the funeral home
with a cup of coffee in my hand
the hand that still smells of Geneviève's perfume.
Geneviève who I just left standing there with my silence.

In the restroom
I'm hiding from my friends who really are trying
who are doing all they can.
It's me who doesn't know what to say to them.

My lips dive into the coffee
and into too many memories.

I drink my coffee black.
My mother always drank hers
with lots of half-and-half.

MATT
I never asked her to give me back her key.
I thought it would be easier if she decided to come back.
I imagined myself coming home one evening
and finding her there
in our apartment
as if nothing had ever happened.

She left at the end of March, on the day of the last snowstorm.
One week after she left
on a Friday when the snow was melting and the city smelled of water

my boss Sylvain came into my office and dropped a key on the papers
on my desk.
"Your ex just came by, Matt, she left this for you."

There was her key lying on top of a pile of paper
a normal brass key just sitting there
not doing anything
no note, nothing
quite small, all on its own, abandoned.

Sylvain told me to take the rest of the day off.
I went back to my place at two in the afternoon
to the apartment that was more empty than ever
and I bought a plane ticket for Sarajevo
leaving on June 4
her birthday.
I would go and look for myself somewhere else.
On the evening of June 3, I gave her a call
left her a message asking her to call me back
then a message telling her I was going to Sarajevo
then a message inviting her to come to Sarajevo with me
then a message begging her to come with me.
She never answered her phone on the evening of June 3.
She never got back to me.
I left on June 4.
On my own.

ELSIE
That morning before the funeral
I drank a cup of coffee in my blue mug
the one with the water lily design that my mother made for me
years ago.

I look at the mug
I think of my mother
I go to the fridge
I take the half-and-half
I pour some in my coffee
a little
then more
then all of it.
My coffee was the same colour as my mother's face.
I didn't drink it
I left it there on the counter.

I went into my bedroom and took a box out of the closet.
Inside it
a tiny pair of children's moccasins with rabbit fur
and another larger pair of moccasins
which had lost nearly all their beads
and with a worn-out left heel.

My mother
when she was writing
liked to take her heel out and swing her moccasin on the end of
her toes
only with her left foot
no idea why.

She'd bought herself some new ones somewhere in Manitoba.
And I had kept the old ones.

They never fit me
my mother's moccasins.
Mine

too small
hers
too big.
Me
in between the two.

MATT
With her pile of mail gone
it's as if even her name had faded away from our apartment
(from my apartment).
My vacation isn't officially over yet
but I can't stay here staring at the walls
thinking of her
thinking of Sarajevo
expecting nothing
expecting nobody.
Tomorrow I'll go back to work.

ELSIE
The coffee at the funeral parlour is disgusting.
My sincere condolences to the catering service.
I pour it in the toilet
I don't cry
I leave the restroom
I avoid Geneviève and the others
I go back home, without saying goodbye to anyone
like when I went to book fairs with my mother.

Four

ELSIE
The hole in the street.

On the first day
police
yellow tape saying DANGER.
On the second day
nothing.
On the third day
the city
orange cones
a sign
DANGER
a brochure for the residents of the street
"Emergency Repair and You."
Be ready to evacuate at any moment if you're asked to
if the DANGER is too great.
On the fourth day
the day after the funeral
a man wearing a white hard hat and carrying surveyor's equipment
on the fifth day
nothing
on the sixth day
nothing

on the seventh day
a new kind of cone.

I'm on leave.
My colleagues from the university call me one at a time.
So do my friends. One at a time.
Geneviève, she calls me every day
always at the same time.

Day eight since my mother's death.
I'm sprawled out on my balcony.
The air is heavy.
The sky is grey
almost white.
In the street: there he is again.
The surveyor surrounded by his team and his trucks.
A child in a sandbox.

He lifts his head in my direction.
His eyes in my eyes.
We look at each other.
Rooted to the spot.
In the distance, you can hear the rumbling of thunder.
The wind is picking up.

A woman from his team goes over to him
taps him on the shoulder
startling him.

He goes off with the woman but first
he gestures to me
a little greeting

with his thumb and two fingers on the edge of his white helmet.
A cowboy surveyor.

MATT
I firmly attach the cables
I buckle on my harness
and I start descending into the gulf.
I'm suspended above the abyss and the red car crashed at the bottom of
the hole.

ELSIE
From my balcony
I hear him shout "Down!"

MATT
I'm in the hole
it's humid
an insect climbs up my boot.
I look up at the sky as it turns darker and darker, shaped by the walls of
the hole.
The storm is approaching.

I'm in the belly of the city.

Here
the disembowelled street
and images of the streets of Sarajevo
one on top of the other.
I touch the walls of the hole
and the earth crumbles under my fingers.

It's a fragile thing, a city
beneath the concrete and the asphalt and the skyscrapers.

ELSIE
From the street
his team lowers a big box down to him.

MATT
Chains, s-hooks, nylon straps tested at six thousand pounds.
I attach the red car.
I check and double-check the chains and the hooks
so there's no DANGER when our crane's ready to pull the car out of
the hole.
The owner of the car's been traced using the papers that were inside.
He came to the city office
took the bag they gave him with the stuff from the car.
But now I look
and under the driver's seat
well hidden
there's a book with a blue-and-white cover.

I get hold of the book, pull it out, look at it.
The image on the cover, under the round stain from a coffee cup:
silhouettes of blue buildings on a white background
like veins.
The title, in a darker blue
Haven
and the name of the author
Gabrielle Sauriol.

Gabrielle Sauriol . . .
Her name on the TV screens at the airport
her car accident
her funeral
she's everywhere just recently.

A note inside the book about the image on the cover says:
"*Sarajevo, impressions.* Drawing by the author."
A first drop of rain slams down right in the middle of the cover.

ELSIE
The surveyor comes back up out of the hole and throws something
into his pickup.
He gives a signal to the others and to the sound of the engines
the red car is lifted up like a rag doll.
From inside the car
pieces of the disintegrated city rain down.

The crane sets the corpse of the car down on a tow truck.
My stomach turns.
All at once, the storm lets loose.
The rain gets heavier and heavier.

The cowboy surveyor gives a signal to his people
and they all move off
crane
tow truck
trucks
everyone goes
leaving behind
the two different kinds of cones
and the yellow police tape (DANGER)
under the pelting rain.

Five

ELSIE
Day nine.
Outside
the area around the hole is swarming with workers wearing city
uniforms
inside
I'm filling the bathtub even though it's sweltering out.

Wallowing in the hot water
I think about sad things
so that I can finally cry
because if I don't cry
it's as if my mother's death didn't
mean
a thing.

Sitting in the bath
I grasp the hot-water faucet with my toes.
A few useless drops then nothing.
Empty pipes.

I plunge my head under the water.

MATT
It's the morning of the ninth day
the ninth day since I got back from Sarajevo.

Things to do. .
Apartment number 2.
I knock on the door.
No response.
On the first page of the pile of papers in my hand
a name jumps out at me.
Occupant of apartment number 2: Sauriol, Elsie.

I knock
harder.

ELSIE
There's a knock at the door and I feel it deep in my chest.

MATT
I knock one last time
with my fist
so that it's loud.
No response.
So I prepare my pink sheet

ELSIE
I get out of the bath

MATT
my Scotch tape

ELSIE
think about putting clothes on
no time

MATT
my signature in blue ink on the pink paper

ELSIE
I'm dripping all over the place

MATT
"Emergency Repair and You"

ELSIE
I open the door

MATT
ELSIE
face to face

ELSIE
the cowboy land surveyor

MATT
the girl from the balcony yesterday
wearing a towel

ELSIE
Yes?

MATT
Er. I'm disturbing you. I'm sorry. Are you Elsie Sauriol, the registered
occupant of this apartment?

ELSIE
That's me.

A long pause. MATT, who has been holding his breath, exhales.

MATT

(flashing a badge) Matt Hamidovic, city engineer. We've had to cut off your water for the day. For repair work.

ELSIE

Can I have another look at your ID?

MATT holds out his badge towards her.

ELSIE

Matej Hamidovic.

MATT

Matt. It's easier.

A long silence.

ELSIE

The whole day?

MATT

We should be able to turn the water back on by the end of the afternoon. We're not doing the real work yet. Not today. Only tests. To find out just how bad the damage is.

ELSIE

Ah.

MATT hands ELSIE a four-litre bottle of water. She doesn't take it.

MATT
And we're also giving everyone four litres of water. Just in case.

ELSIE
In case what?

MATT
In case you haven't stocked up.

ELSIE
The city asked us to in the last flyer.

MATT
You never know. People aren't always so far-sighted.

> *ELSIE doesn't reply. MATT is still holding the bottle of water in his outstretched arm.*

You have to take it in any case. They gave me four bottles of water. There are four apartments.

ELSIE
(taking the bottle) Thank you.

MATT
No problem. Sorry again for disturbing you.

ELSIE
It's fine.

MATT
Have a good day.

ELSIE
You too.

Beat.

MATT
Are you the daughter of Gabrielle Sauriol, the writer? The one who died last week?

Beat.

Sauriol isn't a very common name. And we've been hearing it everywhere recently.

ELSIE
Is that any of your business?

MATT
Er. Yes. No. I—er. I'm sorry. I . . .

Beat.

ELSIE
Okay, well, have a good day.

MATT
I'm really sorry. My sincere condolences.

Beat.

She was your mother, right? You look like her. From what I've seen on TV, I mean. Photos. You look like her.

ELSIE doesn't reply.

MATT
It must be strange to be offered condolences by a stranger. I'm sorry.

ELSIE
If you knew how many strangers have offered me condolences since June 14.

MATT
(uncomfortable) Oh, yes. Right. Sure. It must be lots. I hadn't realized that ... Forgive me. I'm sorry. I didn't want to —

ELSIE
Tell me something about yourself.

MATT
What?

ELSIE
Tell me something interesting about you. So I can feel like I know you. So you're not just another stranger giving me condolences because I'm the daughter of.

MATT
Er. I don't know ... I ... I'm just going to leave. I'm sorry.

ELSIE
Stop apologizing. Just tell me something, anything.

MATT
Anything? Er. Okay . . . I've got a scar on my knee. I don't remember how I got it. I must have been too young . . . A circular scar.

A long pause.

ELSIE
Thanks for the condolences, Matej. Have a good day.

MATT
ELSIE
The door closes.

ELSIE
Standing there in my puddle of water
the towel wrapped around me
it feels to me as if I'm steaming through my pores.

I can feel Matej Hamidovic's eyes all over my face
as if it was written on my skin that my mother's dead
and that my mother was HER.
Matej Hamidovic looked at me as if he was trying to see HER
in my eyes.
I look like her.
Everyone says so.
It must be true.

I open the bottle of water
holding it in both hands
and I drink.

I drink until my stomach hurts
as if I'd never drunk before.
Cold water to prevent my skin from evaporating.

MATT
I can still feel Elsie Sauriol's eyes on me.
I stay there for a moment, not moving,
looking at the closed door of apartment number 2.

In the corridor, I notice a really strong smell
I'm bombarded by an aroma
coriander
I'm almost certain
it's coriander.

My eyes fill up with tears.
It smells so strong it almost has a colour.
I blink
and then nothing.
The smell has disappeared.

It must be coming from one of the other apartments
someone who's cooking something with coriander.
I knock on the other doors
without getting any response
nobody home.

I wipe my eyes.
Strange.

I leave the pink flyers stuck on the other three doors.
I stop thinking about it.

Six

ELSIE
Afternoon.
No water.

I lie down on the floor of the living room.
From here I can see all the dustballs under the sofa
the rings on the coffee table
the hairs made to dance on the floor by the open window.
From here I can see the mess.

I feel like moving,
I feel like getting out of my own skin.
Housework. I could do some housework.
In any case
that's what you're supposed to do, right,
after the death of your mother?

I get up from the floor.
On the shelf above my desk
lined up one next to another
my mother's books
all first editions with inscriptions
always the same thing.

"*To my dear Elsie. For everything.*"

I run my fingers along them
I don't even know if I've opened all of them
I always use other copies of her books for teaching
other copies in which I've written notes
whose pages I've folded over.

Housework.

My mother's desk was always very tidy.
The untidy writer's desk is a cliché.
On my desk
papers pile up in parallel stacks
graded papers
class plans
letters to colleagues.

I could start the housework here.
Old copies of dissertations from last term
face down on the desk.
I pick up the one on top:
"The Theme of Travel in Gabrielle Sauriol's *Haven*."
I give up on the idea of housework
and go and stretch out on the lounger in the sun.

MATT
Leaning my back against my truck,
I think about Elsie Sauriol in apartment number 2.
I take out my phone
open up Google
type in "Gabrielle Sauriol"
and get into Wikipedia

I quickly read through her bio
the books she's written, the prizes she's won.
No mention anywhere of her having a daughter.
I put my phone back in my pocket.
I pick up the book, which has been lying on the passenger seat
since the day we got the car out of the hole.

ELSIE
He's still there outside
the land surveyor
no
the engineer
Matej Hamidovic
Matt-it's-easier Hamidovic
Matt Hamidovic with his round scar on his knee
leaning against his truck.
He's holding a book in his hand
and he's reading the back cover
a white-and-blue book I'd recognize anywhere.

MATT
I look up and see her looking at me
Elsie Sauriol
sitting on her balcony.
I put the book back in my truck
I go round to the door on the driver's side
I turn the key in the ignition.
I look up towards the balcony.
No one there.

ELSIE
I go into the bathroom
I sit on the edge of the tub

I turn on the cold water.
The faucet protests and makes banging noises
then spits out the water that's come back on.
I turn off the faucet.
I sit in the empty tub.
I hear Matej Hamidovic's truck turn the corner and drive away.

Seven

MATT
I wake up sweating at 4:55 in the morning.
I rub my eyes to get rid of the images of Sarajevo.
My heart's beating too fast
I feel warm but I'm shivering
blood pounding in my temples.

I've been having nightmares since I got back from Sarajevo
I can no longer sleep through the night without waking up.

The stories they tell you in Sarajevo
when you say that you too come from Sarajevo
when you say you're looking for your parents
that you're looking for your memories.
People think they're helping you
people want to help you.
They tell you their stories
and they all stay in your head
all melted into each other.

I throw the sheets to the foot of the bed
turn on the bedside lamp and the room is bathed in a yellowish light.
In that light
the scar on my knee looks even more hollow.
I put my thumb in the round hole on my knee.

My thumb fits perfectly inside my scar
like my thumb fit perfectly
into the bullet holes made by the snipers in the walls of Sarajevo.

On the bedside table
the book from the car.
I open it.
"There are some moments that are beyond us."
First sentence on the first page of the first chapter.

I close the book.
I turn out the light and try to get back to sleep.
No point.
5:17.
I reach for my phone and open my email.
Right at the top there's a message from Sanel Catic
my interpreter from Sarajevo:
"Still nothing, Matej," he writes.
"I'll keep looking.
We'll find something about them eventually."

I give up on the idea of sleeping.
I get up and get dressed to go for a run and watch the sun come up.

Eight

ELSIE
Day ten, afternoon.
Tasks accomplished:
vacuuming
deleting, without listening to them, the eleven voicemails from
Geneviève
looking out the window to see what progress has been made with
the hole
which is to say none at all.

I decide to go somewhere else to see if that's where I am.
It's the first time I've left my place since the funeral.

I go into a café
the café I go to all the time
and order a pot of black coffee.
The patio is full of students sitting under the umbrellas.
Familiar and unfamiliar faces.
Talking in low voices as they look in my direction.

MATT
I've been awake since 4:55 in the morning.
I went out for a run
took a shower
put in my normal work day

came back home and once there
I wander around my empty apartment.
I let the hours go by.
I pick up the book that's lying on the bed.
The drawing on the cover depicting buildings in Sarajevo.
I recognize them because I was there.

I open *Haven*.
To read it properly.
Take in all the words, all the images.
A mother loses her daughter
a photojournalist shot dead in the streets of Sarajevo.
When the war is finally over
years later
the mother leaves for Sarajevo to meet up with Adnan, a journalist
who worked with her
daughter
and to see the place where her daughter died
to make her peace with that
to understand
or at least to feel the same ground her daughter felt under her feet as
she died.

ELSIE
Years ago
my thesis advisor asked me why I wanted to become a professor of
literature.
I replied by saying
something coherent
no doubt
something like, To shape young minds, promote critical thinking,
discovery.

I do like teaching
it's true.

But sometimes I think I became a literature professor so I could teach
my mother's novels and feel like she was always there.

Before *Haven*
the two of us together
after *Haven*
me, fourteen years old, waiting
at Marilynne and Jeff's
at Jean-François and Sophie's
at Fabien and Peter's
at Yasmina's
and her everywhere without me.

Waiting for her to come back
that's all I ever did.

I love and I detest *Haven*.

MATT
They did offer to take me to Sarajevo
my parents from here.

They offered that to me
when I was twelve
then fifteen
then nineteen
and every time
I said
no.

I said I wasn't ready.
So they stopped offering.

On June 4, I left on my own
without telling them.

I called them from Sarajevo to tell them where I was.
Their reaction was perfect
they didn't ask me
why now
why on your own.

Basically they knew that by leaving on June 4
my ex's birthday
I was running away from something.
I said goodbye
told them not to worry
that I was fine.
I logged out of Skype
disconnected the computer
and looked out of the window of the room I'd rented
the roofs of the city
the streets
swarming with people
the sun that day
the Miljacka River criss-crossed with bridges.
I let myself drift off to sleep
to catch up on the six hours of jet lag.

That was the last time I really slept.

ELSIE

I put my empty cup on the counter and leave.

On the door next to the café
a blue-and-green sign
"Librairie Pelletier et Fille."
I go through the door not really looking
for anything.

The "daughter" of Pelletier et Fille is busy arranging books on a shelf
she sees me
she smiles at me
she knows me
I come here a lot.
I see her stand up as if to come over to me but she changes her mind
she carries on arranging the books.
She doesn't know what to say.
Nobody knows what to say.

I move away so it's easier for her to avoid me
then further in at the back of the bookstore
right in front of me
a large colour photograph of my mother.

Under the big picture
the year of my mother's birth and the year of her death.

My mother, who has a date of death.

On a table at the foot of the photo
my mother's books

the same ones I have at home
but in multiple copies
Haven and all the others
new and used
first editions
paperback editions
translations.
All that's left of my mother now
is that.

MATT
I was in Sarajevo to find traces of my biological parents.
I walked from office to office
from counter to counter
from official to official
with my interpreter Sanel, who follows me everywhere because I've
forgotten everything.

I've erased even the simplest words.

Mom and Dad
mama i tata

Mom and Dad
Nicole Clark and Alain Vallier.

ELSIE
I take all the books
I make a huge pile, balancing precariously
I make my way to the checkout
I put everything down on the counter.

"Madame Sauriol?"
The face of one of my students from last winter term
Samuel Rogers-Martin
long hair
baseball cap
burgundy Doc Martens
staring at me.

The books: I want all of them
the new ones, the used ones, the ones in French, in English, in German,
Italian, Arabic, all of them
they're mine now
I want them to belong to me
all of them
pieces of my mother.
It's all that's left of her
I have the right to them.

I hand my credit card to Samuel Rogers-Martin
so he can see I'm serious.

Fwoosht goes the credit card.

MATT
Near the end of the novel
there's a sentence that hits me.
The mother asks Adnan
the journalist who worked with her daughter
what he's going to do now that the war is over.
Adnan replies:
"Sarajevo, it's not a place for me anymore."

The mother tells him she's sorry
Adnan asks her why
she says she doesn't know.

ELSIE
Samuel Rogers-Martin hesitates for a moment.
I know what he's going to say.
Like the others.
Like all the others.
My body tenses up.
Samuel Rogers-Martin looks at the counter:

"I liked your course this winter so much, Madame Sauriol. You really are the best professor I've had in the department."

My shoulders relax.

"I'm sorry you're going through this. My sincerest condolences, Madame Sauriol."

He says all that very quickly, as if he was afraid of my reaction
as if he wanted to get it over with as quickly as possible.
I look at him
and I believe him.
He's the first person I believe when he tells me he's sorry.

Thank you
I say and I believe that too.

Samuel Rogers-Martin packs up all my books in two cloth bags with the Pelletier et Fille logo.

And I leave
on foot
with my mother in my outstretched arms.

Nine

ELSIE
I bought
thirty-seven of my mother's books at Pelletier et Fille
fourteen at a chain bookstore
twenty-one at the campus bookstore
eighteen online
and I went to get the dozen or so that were in my office at the
university.
Day fourteen.
I took the books out of the bags and lined them all up against one of
the walls in the living room.

MATT
Apartment 2. Elsie Sauriol.
I knock on the door with another pink flyer from the city.

ELSIE opens the door.

ELSIE
Yes?

MATT
(handing her a flyer) Here's a schedule for the repair work. We won't
start before seven o'clock during the week and eight o'clock on

Saturday and Sunday because it's a residential street. If you have any questions, you can call this number.

ELSIE
That makes no difference to me. I'm at home all the time in any case.

MATT
My job is to hand out the flyer and let people know.

ELSIE
Okay.

A long pause. They look at each other, as if they were holding their breath.

Come in.

MATT
Why?

ELSIE
I wanted to apologize. For the other day. I know you meant well when you offered me your condolences. I was just . . . worn out.

MATT
I understand. It's fine. No problem. I'm sorry.

ELSIE
Come in.

MATT enters.

MATT
Thank you.

Beat.

ELSIE
What do you do all day leaning against your truck looking into the hole? There's nobody there, no crane, no other trucks, just you. What do you do all day, Matej Hamidovic, city engineer? What are you looking at in that hole?

MATT
What about you, what do you do all day, Elsie Sauriol?

ELSIE
I'm on bereavement leave, following union rules.

Beat.

Coffee?

MATT
Okay.

ELSIE goes off towards the kitchen.

(in a louder voice) With a little milk if you have some.

ELSIE comes back with two cups of coffee.

Thanks.

He sips his coffee and looks around.

You have a lot of books.

ELSIE
I'm a lecturer at the university. In Canadian literature.

MATT
I just read *Haven*. For the first time. I didn't know anything about it. I was in Sarajevo two weeks ago. It's a weird coincidence that I happened upon *Haven* now, don't you think?

Beat. ELSIE doesn't reply.

You're lucky to have had Gabrielle Sauriol as your mother. If you think about it, it's as if your mother could never really die. Traces of her will always remain for you. It must be good to have that at least.

Beat.

I'm sorry. I'm talking too much again. Saying the wrong things.

ELSIE
It's all right.

Beat.

"Hamidovic," that's Yugoslavian, right?

MATT
Why do you want to know?

ELSIE
So I get to know you. If I have to see you every day in my street, I'd like to know who you are. You know I'm the daughter of . . . Everyone

knows I'm the daughter of. People think they know me, think they know things about me because of that. I decided I'm going to get to know people for real.

MATT
Er. Okay. I came here when I was nine years old. When the war was about to end and the siege was lifted, the Red Cross came to Sarajevo. They say I was found in the street eating from garbage cans. All I remembered was my name. I couldn't remember my address, my telephone number, nothing. They put me in a Red Cross orphanage. I stayed there for a year and a half but I don't remember any of it. Nine years totally wiped out. My earliest memory is of my first day here, with my adoptive parents. It's as if there'd never been anything before that.

ELSIE
Maybe it's better that way.

MATT
The couple who adopted me, Alain and Nicole, had spent years on the waiting list for a baby. I don't know if they were disappointed. If they'd have preferred something else.

ELSIE
Disappointed?

MATT
It's hard, adopting a grown child.

ELSIE
They didn't give you their name? Your parents from here?

MATT

They wanted me to keep my name. They thought that was going to help me to remember. I hate my name. It constantly reminds me of what's missing from my life. If I was called Matt Vallier, there'd be no problem.

Beat.

ELSIE

Did you ever have a dog?

MATT

A dog?

ELSIE

When I met people for the first time, they always asked me what my mother was doing, what she was working on. No one ever asked questions about me.

Beat.

What she's doing right now . . . right now she's drowning . . .

MATT

(visibly uncomfortable) I can leave if you want. If you want to be on your own.

ELSIE

(pulling herself together) It's my turn to know things about people. Did you ever have a dog?

MATT takes out his phone, finds a photo, and shows it to ELSIE.

MATT

Yes, when I was fifteen. A black Labrador named Max. That's Max before he died. He's really old in that one. He died last summer.

ELSIE

Did you cry when he died?

MATT

(putting away his phone) That's normal, isn't it? I cried a bit and I took two days off, told them I was sick.

ELSIE

Two days?

MATT

The union doesn't give you time off when your dog dies.

Beat.

ELSIE

Where is he now, your dog?

MATT

The vet gives you a box with your pet's ashes in it. That's how it works. My dog's ashes are buried at my parents' because that was his first home.

ELSIE

If people ask me where my mother is now, what should I say? In the Pacific, being dismembered by orcas, pecked at by crabs, wound up in seaweed, scratched by the salt, lured down into the depths . . .

Beat.

That's macabre. I'm sorry, that's not what you came here for.

MATT
It's okay . . .

ELSIE
Come back. Tomorrow if you like. For a coffee.

MATT
(giving his cup back to ELSIE*)* Okay. Have a good day, Elsie.

> ELSIE *closes the door.* MATT *remains standing alone in the corridor.*

The taste of coffee still in my mouth.
Standing there in the corridor
with its beige walls
and four doors all blue
the same blue as on the cover of *Haven*.

I blink and the walls of the corridor become riddled with bullets
the floor is covered with debris, pieces of glass
my nostrils get filled up with a smell like burnt plastic
I fall to the floor
my knee's covered in blood.
I scream with pain.
I blink and the hardwood floor becomes a wine-red carpet
there's a faint smell of coriander in the air
a distant voice murmurs my name
"Matej Matty Matty"
and there's a woman's laugh.

I laugh too.
It's a small child's laugh but I know it's me.

I blink and everything vanishes
and it's the corridor in Elsie Sauriol's building
clean
beige
silent.

I get back up
feeling nauseous
my hands moist and trembling.

The door of apartment number 2 stays closed
as if nothing had happened
nothing at all.
I didn't scream, didn't laugh
not really.

I go back to my truck
I go back home.

My empty apartment crushes me.

My empty apartment
my empty bed
me
just a little more empty
since I came back from Sarajevo.

Ten

ELSIE

Lying on the floor
I look at all the copies of *Haven* lined up against the living-room wall.

MATT

I turn on my computer
I type
Gabrielle Sauriol
and I read
in English, French, German, which I have a smattering of because of
my ex.

I open pages in Bosnian
in Croatian
in Serbian
just to see the words that I could understand if things had been
different.

ELSIE

The *ding* of a text message: Geneviève.
"Are you hungry?"
I don't reply.
Ding.
"You have to eat."
Ding.

"Should I bring something to your place? I could be there in twenty
minutes."
Ding.
"Elsie. Come on."
I don't reply.
The texts stop.

MATT
Articles
interviews
features
her website
her Twitter account
her Facebook page.
Mind-boggling.

I want to hear her voice.
It's easy to find it in the CBC Radio archives.
She's given tons of interviews.

ELSIE
I'm sitting on the floor with my laptop on my legs
and the CBC Radio archives open, I'm listening to one of my mother's
interviews.
Maybe if I hear her voice
I'll manage to cry.

She talks. She answers questions.
I listen.

I don't recognize her voice in the CBC interview.
It's her special-occasion voice
not her real voice.

I don't cry.

MATT
Elsie has the same voice as her mother.
I've got forty-four Google tabs open
biographies
articles she wrote
articles others wrote about her
photos
Gabrielle Sauriol at the University of Victoria
Gabrielle Sauriol at the National Arts Centre
Gabrielle Sauriol visiting the Académie française

ELSIE
The phone rings.
I know without looking that it's Geneviève.
I let it ring
then silence
then the beep of the message left in my voicemail.
Now that my mother's not here anymore
Geneviève is the only person who uses my voicemail.

MATT
On the twenty-second page of results
I find a poorly framed and blurry photo:
Gabrielle Sauriol and her daughter Elsie Sauriol, Ph.D. student at the
University of Ottawa.

ELSIE
I play another interview
then another
in English, in French, one on the radio, one on TV.
Always the same artificial voice.

A voice I don't recognize.
I close out of everything.
I fling the computer onto the sofa.

MATT
I can follow the whole career
the whole life of Gabrielle Sauriol
in my forty-four Google tabs.

Traces of Gabrielle Sauriol everywhere . . .
Nearly ten million results.
It feels good to look for someone who can really be found.

I turn off the sound
I close out of everything
and I open a new page
I type in
Elsie Sauriol
1,155 results
mostly her articles about literature
and photos that aren't of her
except the one with her mother.

I type in my name
and the first page that comes up
is the one for the city's planning department.
I look.
Even on Google
I don't exist in Sarajevo.

I delete everything.
I type in the name of my ex
945 results

I go through the photos one at a time
I spend too long looking at them
I turn off the computer.

I turn out all the lights
outside a flash of lightning splits the sky
I blink and my walls are covered in bullet holes
my nose fills up with a strong smell of dust
the air is electric
and my hands tremble.
I blink and everything returns to normal.

Another flash of lightning
a thunderclap like a bomb
and the storm breaks
violently.
I go out into the street
I let myself get drenched to the bone.

I go back in and type in my ex's phone number
she picks up
her voice goes right through me
I hang up.
She doesn't call back.
Neither do I.

I read *Haven* again, from the beginning.

ELSIE
If I'd known
I'd have recorded my mother's voice
not the one she used when receiving a prize
not the one she used when giving master classes

or the one in her interviews or on her website.

I'd have recorded her real voice.

The one from before *Haven*.

Eleven

ELSIE
Day sixteen.
The hole is still there
shaped like a hole.
A truck from the city
and Matej Hamidovic getting out of it.

MATT
Apartment number 2. Elsie Sauriol.
I knock on the door.

ELSIE
Yes?

MATT
Hello.

ELSIE
Come in.

MATT
(handing her a bag) I've got something for you. They were getting rid
of them at the main library so I picked them up for your collection on
the floor. Three copies of *Haven* and two others.

ELSIE
(taking the bag) They're getting rid of them?

MATT
The librarian told me they'd bought new editions. They were going to send these ones to Pelletier et Fille.

ELSIE
(looking at the bag) Thanks.

MATT
You're welcome.

    Beat.

ELSIE
Coffee?

MATT
I can't, sorry. I have to go. It's crazy right now. A subcontractor didn't show up. I have to make some calls, find a replacement.

ELSIE
Okay.

MATT
Next time.

    He heads towards the door.

ELSIE
Wait!

MATT
(turning back) What is it?

ELSIE
Do you think everyone has a moment in their life where it's as if a hole just opened up in front of them? A moment before and a moment after? Do you think everyone has a scar in their timeline? Like me: before and after my mother's death . . .

MATT
It's hard to say, I didn't know you before.

ELSIE
Did you know that my mother never went to Sarajevo to write *Haven*? She went afterwards, for conferences, for master classes, even one time to receive an honorary doctorate from the University of Sarajevo. But to write *Haven*, never.

MATT
Two weeks ago was the first time I'd gone back to Sarajevo. I wanted to find my biological parents.

ELSIE
And?

MATT
Nothing for the moment. I'm still looking.

ELSIE
The hole outside, it's the before and the after of the street. You're going to repair the hole you'll patch it up so it looks nice but there's always going to be a scar, a trace of the repair work. And that part of the asphalt will always be a little weaker, a little more breakable.

MATT
It's true.

ELSIE
I'd like it if my mother's death was like a real scar on my body, a real mark on my skin, something concrete.

Beat.

Can I see your knee?

MATT lifts the leg of his pants and shows her the scar on his knee, just for a very short moment.

MATT
Nothing special.

ELSIE
But you'll always be able to remember that day.

MATT
Actually, I don't remember it. For me, it's as if it had always been there.

Beat.

Tomorrow's Canada Day, so there won't be any repair work until Friday at the earliest. Monday maybe.

He takes a pink flyer out of his pocket.

Oh, yes. This is for the residents. To explain that the work's been pushed back.

ELSIE takes the flyer.

ELSIE
Thank you. And thanks for the books.

MATT
It was no trouble.

Beat.

ELSIE takes a book from the pile in the living room and gives it to MATT.

ELSIE
Before you leave. Take this one.

MATT
What is it?

ELSIE
One of her short-story collections. She wrote it before *Haven*. People don't know that because it was published after. It's really different; you notice it right away. It's my favourite.

MATT
Thanks. I'll read it.

ELSIE
I hope so.

Beat.

MATT
I have to go, I'm sorry. Have a good day.

ELSIE
Same to you.

MATT
ELSIE
The door closes.

MATT
I leave the half-light of the beige corridor and go outside.
The sun is dazzling.
With one hand I look in my pockets for my sunglasses
with the other, the one holding Elsie's book,
I shade my eyes.

I'm smelling gasoline
and on the asphalt
I see rainbows of oil shining in the puddles.
I feel the rain falling
and an icy cold in my bones.
In the distance, gunshots
and a man lying on the ground at my feet.
The cold, the rain, the man . . .
Nausea
dizziness.

At last I get hold of my sunglasses and put them on.

Everything vanishes.
The puddles, the gasoline, the rain, the cold, the man on the ground.
Sun. Humidity. Breeze. Nothing out of the ordinary.

One of my guys is looking at me.
"You okay, man? You're white as a sheet."
I'm okay
I tell him
yes I'm fine, yes.

I throw the short stories into my truck.
I wipe my hands on my pants.
I catch my breath.

ELSIE
I line up the five books I got from Matej Hamidovic with the others on
the floor.
I go into the bathroom
I run the hot water
and I get into the tub and make a boat out of the pink flyer from
the city.
My paper boat floats on the scalding-hot water.
I'd like it if it caught fire.

I get hold of the faucet with my foot.
Make the bath hotter still.
I want it to hurt.
If I really hurt myself
would my mother come back to take care of me?

The pink boat gets saturated with water and slowly sinks to the bottom
of the bath like my drowned mother.

One of my memories:
the last time I saw my mother
one month before the accident.

She was staying with me for two days before leaving for Toronto then
on to San Francisco.
She was lying in my bed and I was stretched out on the sofa in the
living room.
I could hear her breathing and her moans through the open doors
because my mother never slept well.

One of my memories:
sitting at the table in my kitchen
eating a mushroom omelette
opposite my tired-looking mother drowning her coffee with cream.

Why don't you sleep, Mom?
Why don't you ever sleep?
Stop for a moment
settle down somewhere
so we can go back to being together
like before
before *Haven*
before the prizes and the editors and the book fairs and the sales fig-
ures and the conferences and the colloquia and the translations and the
round tables and the film producers and all these people who take you
and tear you out of my life
stay here
with me.

I remember I wanted to say all that to her.
I remember I didn't say anything.

Twelve

ELSIE
Day nineteen.
Saturday morning, lying around in bed.
Like a normal person on a Saturday morning.
But on bereavement leave
Saturday morning or Thursday afternoon or Monday evening or
Wednesday at four in the morning
who cares
because it's all the same.

ELSIE
MATT
Saturday morning, the phone rings.

ELSIE
It's a number I don't recognize
it's not the usual time for Geneviève to call
I don't know what to do so I pick up.

MATT
Elsie? It's Matt Hamidovic, from the city. Did I wake you?

ELSIE
No.

Beat.

Is there a problem? Do we have to evacuate?

MATT
No.

ELSIE
How'd you get my phone number?

MATT
It's in the papers I have. In case.

Beat.

What was it like? Living with her.

ELSIE
You want to talk about my mother? Why? You read *Haven* and you feel... what? A deep connection with Gabrielle Sauriol? As if she understood you? As if she'd put your biggest existential questions down on paper?

What do you want me to tell you? You want me to talk about my mother the writer? You want me to tell you what colour the walls of her study were? How she drank her coffee? For me to tell you she didn't like the film version of *Haven* even though she pretended it was brilliant when anyone asked her about it? Tell you about the ideas she had for novels that she'll never write now? Is that what you want?

Or do you want me to tell you about all the times her friend Jeff drove us to the airport and how I tried not to cry on the way back when she was taking off for Paris or Brussels or New York and leaving me here all alone? Or do you want to hear about my sixteenth birthday, which I spent with her friend Yasmina because Gabrielle Sauriol absolutely had to go to London? Or about my Ph.D. graduation, which she'd promised to come to and which I didn't attend myself after she'd called me the day before to tell me she had to stay in Vancouver? Do you want me to tell you about all the friends, work colleagues, fans who were more important than me? Do you want me to make you a list of all the times when I needed my mother, her words, her answers, her arms, and she wasn't there, as if she'd decided when I was fourteen that I didn't need her anymore?

Tell me, Matej Hamidovic, what do you want to know?

MATT
I apologize. I had to ask. I had to know. She's everywhere, your mother. Mine is nowhere.

Beat.

ELSIE
When I was little, my mother had a big green book that was always lying around in the kitchen: *The Birds of North America.* And when she saw a bird, she would point it out to me and say: "It's a cedar waxwing," "It's a brown-headed cowbird," "It's a common yellowthroat." And I didn't care. I so didn't care. Birds . . . they were her thing. But yesterday, looking out of the window, I saw a bird in a tree, and I said to myself: "Look, Elsie, it's a mourning warbler." Things like that . . . coming back to the surface. Being reminded of the name of that bird. When I thought "mourning warbler," it was as if I heard my mother's voice.

A long silence.

MATT
You still there?

ELSIE
What would you do to be able to meet your biological parents?

MATT
What do you mean?

ELSIE
If you could, would you give up one of your senses? Would you lie down on hot coals? Would you exchange the lives of all the dogs you'll have in the future? Do you say to yourself: if I'd been a better person, maybe they'd be here with me? Do you ask yourself: if I hadn't been this or that, would things be different? If my mother had worn her seat belt, would she have survived? Would she have become a vegetable, not capable of writing anymore, lying in a bed, hooked up to machines? Would I have had to live with the decision to unplug her? Would that be worse than now?

A long pause.

Your mother from here, what does she do?

MATT
She runs a chain of health-food stores. My father's an engineer too. Computer engineer. I wanted to work with real things: rocks, wood, metal, solid things.

One time, I came across an interview with a violinist in the Sarajevo symphony orchestra who'd lost both his sons during the siege. The article explained how he was still looking for them because he'd never seen them dead. He'd never seen their bodies, so he refused to believe they were dead. The story of that violinist . . .

ELSIE
. . . haunts you.

MATT
Did you know that if you google your mother's name you get nearly ten million results?

A long pause.

You want to go get a coffee? Go outside a bit, get some fresh air?

ELSIE
Not today.

MATT
Okay. Another time.

ELSIE
Another time.

MATT
Have a good Saturday.

ELSIE
You too.

She hangs up.

I wrap myself up in the sheet.
I get out of bed and drag the sheet behind me.

I stretch out on the old floor of the living room in front of the books
lined up along the wall.

More than ten million results . . .
I can't get my mind around it:
more than ten million virtual fragments of my mother.
The number makes me feel dizzy.

I run my finger along the edges of the books
there's an empty space
a hole
for the book I loaned to Matej Hamidovic.

Another piece of my mother that's missing.

I don't know how
but I fall asleep on the floor
with my head resting on my hand.
I wake up when I hear someone knocking at the door.
The sun has moved on the floor
it's not morning anymore.

I get up and open the door
face to face
with Geneviève.

We look at each other for a long time
in silence.

I open my mouth
I breathe in
to speak
but she throws herself at me.

"No, Elsie, I don't know what it's like to lose your mother.
To lose your mother when it's the only family you have.
I don't know what it's like to be in so much pain.
I don't know what you're feeling
but I want to help you
and I want you to stop ignoring me
we've known each other too long for that.
Talk or don't talk; that's not important.
Cry or laugh or shout or don't do anything; it doesn't matter.
But let me be with you."

Geneviève comes in.
She does as she usually does
sits on the sofa
throws the cushion she hates onto the floor
crosses her legs under her.
I sit with her
I take the cushion she threw on the floor
and I put it behind my head.
We look at my mother's books lined up along the wall of the
living room.

"There's one missing," she says.

I know, I answer.

"You'll have to take care of that."

I know.

She gets up and goes to the kitchen.
I can hear her making a mess in my cabinets
grinding coffee

running water.
She comes back, sits down again.

I'm sorry, Geneviève.
I didn't want to—
I'm—

"It's fine."

I lean my head against her shoulder
and we stay there in silence
for all of Saturday afternoon.

Thirteen

MATT

Day twenty-one.

Monday morning, 7 a.m. exactly, to the sound of the cranes.

Apartment number 2.

I knock.

ELSIE

MATT

The door opens.

MATT

Just to let you know the water's going to be shut off until at least 2 p.m. today for the repair work. I don't want to disturb you . . . I—

They look at each other.

ELSIE

My bereavement leave is over. Officially I go back to work today. But I turned my computer on and checked my email and I stopped there. And since then I haven't been able to move. I turned my computer on, checked my email, and that's all.

When my mother travelled, she always sent me her itineraries electronically. I collected them. I put a little star next to them because it was important.

I've got twenty-seven emails like that, just from this year. Twenty-seven times when I knew exactly where she was while I was here.

I decided not to work today. I called in sick.

Long pause.

MATT
I think I'm having visions.

ELSIE
Visions?

MATT
Since I got back from Sarajevo. Visions of the war. Or visions from before. Not just images. There are smells, sounds, voices. It's like when you see something moving out of the corner of your eye. You turn around and it disappears. It's as if— I'm sorry. It's ridiculous. I don't know why I'm saying this. I've been sleeping really badly recently, having nightmares, I'm tired, I . . .

ELSIE
I can't cry.

MATT
What?

ELSIE
It's awful, isn't it? I ought to cry. She was my mother.

Beat.

How do you know where he is, your dog? Where is Max?

MATT
I put a big white rock in that spot. And my mother planted flowers round it.

ELSIE
It must be nice.

MATT
It is nice.

ELSIE
I'd like to have my book back.

MATT
Okay.

Beat.

You mean now?

ELSIE
I need it.

MATT
It's in the truck. Let me finish my calls and you can come down with me to get it.

ELSIE
Okay.

MATT
I'll be back.

ELSIE remains on her own.

ELSIE
I close the door behind Matej Hamidovic.
I go into the living room and run my finger along all the books.
Haven with its white cover
all the other books multicoloured.
I dust them with the bottom of my T-shirt.
Books creaking with newness
and books falling to pieces
worn out by too much love.
I inhale them with deep breaths
the smell of the paper
the smell of the glue
a smell in which the new intermingles with the old.
That smell that makes me think of my mother
and her whole life devoted to writing
and my whole life devoted to reading and reading and teaching.
A smell of paper that lingers on my hands.

The sun coming through the window brings all the dust to light
the dust that keeps building up
the dirt from the work outside
the ordinary dust of my life
hairs scattered around
flakes of my skin
particles of me
fragments of the city.

I take deep breaths in the warm air of my living room.
I wonder if anything in my apartment retained the smell of my mother.
A gentle knock on the door.
Matej.

I put my sandals on without fastening them,
I go down to Matej's truck to get my book.
Back at my place
I slide the story collection into the empty space.

I think about Max the dog.
Max the dog always in exactly the place where they left him
under the big white rock
surrounded with flowers.

I think about my mother
about the Pacific Ocean, too big, too vast, too far away from here.

From the living-room window
I see a ruby-throated hummingbird flitting around in the flowers on
the balcony next door.
I hear my mother's voice:
"A ruby-throated hummingbird" . . .
Hours go by.

Fourteen

MATT
Lunch break.
On my phone, right at the top of the inbox:
a message from Sanel Catic
scans of translated documents.
Official documents bearing the seal of the Bosnia–Herzegovinian government and ancient seals
those of the government of Yugoslavia.

"Hi Matej!"
writes Sanel.

"Here are translations of the documents you'll get in the mail in the next few days. Good leads but bad news. I'm sorry, my friend."

Yugoslavia is sending me
a birth certificate:
mine.
My name printed on a typewriter floats just above the line
and under my name, those of my parents:
Jasko Hamidovic
born in Sarajevo, 1957
Zifa Qukovci
born in Belgrade, 1956.

They have names
they exist.
They have names, birthdates, an address, ages, jobs
it's printed on my birth certificate
it's printed.
My parents:
Belgrade and Sarajevo
when there wasn't a war.

Another document.
In a letter of just a few lines
Bosnia–Herzegovina informs me that the exhaustive research they've
carried out has not enabled them to find my parents.

"Disappeared" is the official word
nestali
no death certificate
no document to confirm
anything
just that word
nestali.

"40,000 disappeared in the former Yugoslavia
28,000 during the siege of Sarajevo"
says the translation by Sanel Catic
says the official document.
My two who disappeared
were two among 40,000.

And the 39,998 others
if people can remember them
did they disappear a little less?

I forgot everything.
I made them disappear a second time.

I stretch out on the lawn in the sun.
One of the guys asks me
"You okay, Matt?"

Yes, I just need a minute.

"No problem. Tell us when you want us to start up again."

On the ground
an ant climbs onto my arm
the sound of birds
wind in the leaves
insects buzzing.
I try to remember
my mother's voice
my father's smell
my mother's face
my father's hands
my father's legs
my mother's eyes
fragments
pieces
anything.
And nothing.

Stretched out in the sun
red under my eyelids
the face I see
is Elsie Sauriol's

and the voice I hear
is Gabrielle Sauriol's.

I think about my parents
Alain and Nicole
I wonder what it would have been like to have really been their child
to have known them for the first nine years of my life
I'm sure I'd have loved them even more
I'm sure my parents over there
Jasko and Zifa
would have loved them too.
I imagine them being friends.

I get back up.
I go towards the cranes.
Elsie Sauriol is on her balcony watching me.

ELSIE
Matej Hamidovic is stretched out on the grass, his phone in his hand.
It's really hot. Maybe he felt faint. Needed water. Something.
But he gets up again.
"You okay?"
I say to him
without making a sound, just moving my lips.

MATT
I nod yes with my head in Elsie's direction.
We look at each other for a second or perhaps for an eternity.

All right, guys. Let's get back to it.

ELSIE
The rest of the afternoon
the noise of cranes
hours go by
I watch Matej Hamidovic walking around among his engineer's toys
talking to his team
putting on and taking off his white helmet
drinking water
eating an apple.
Then I see him filling out paperwork while everyone leaves one at
a time.
I see him walk to the door of the building and come in.

MATT
Apartment number 2.
I go in

ELSIE
without knocking.

MATT enters.

MATT
Your water?

ELSIE
Back on. Are you done for the day?

MATT
Yes.

They look at each other without saying anything, then ELSIE
goes towards the kitchen.

ELSIE
Ice?

MATT
Okay.

ELSIE comes back with two glasses of whisky, on the rocks.

MATT
Thanks.

He takes a gulp.

How do you manage to teach literature? Tell me how you spend your life with so little that's concrete, with so few real answers.

I like math, that's just the way I am. I've always liked math. A differential equation, it's always the same. It always functions in the same way and at the end you have an answer. A real answer. The only possible answer. It does you good, a real answer. Things that are vague . . . I have a really hard time with anything that's vague.

He drinks another mouthful. A long silence. MATT goes to sit on the floor, in front of the piles of Gabrielle Sauriol's books. ELSIE sits down with him.

ELSIE
I need help with things that are concrete.

MATT
Pardon?

ELSIE

I need my mother to not just be a body that's sunk to the bottom of the ocean, a body lost in too much water. I need her to be near me, to not have gone off again, to not yet again be at the other end of the world. I want her with me.

MATT

What are you going to do?

ELSIE

There are too many pieces of my mother everywhere. In the ten million results on Google, in the journals doing retrospectives about her career, in all the people she spent more time with than she did with me, in the millions of pages covered with her words. There are so many pieces of my mother that don't belong to me. But the books, those ones, I can do something with those.

You'll repair the hole in the asphalt and a scar will always remain. We'll always be able to remember the accident. That's going to be my mother's tomb.

MATT empties his glass in one gulp.

MATT

I'll help you.

ELSIE

You'd do that for me?

MATT

If that's your answer, I'll help you find it. The worst thing is not knowing. The worst thing is to have done everything you were supposed to

do, to have asked all the right people the right questions, and to still
not have any answer.

Beat.

ELSIE
You didn't find anything?

MATT
Nothing much.

ELSIE
I'm sorry to hear that.

Beat.

MATT
Tonight, come down to the street with your books.

ELSIE
At 2:21 a.m.

MATT
Okay. At 2:21.

A long pause. MATT gives his empty glass to ELSIE.

See you later.

ELSIE
(left on her own) I take my phone and send a text message to
Geneviève.

"I know what I have to do now. Thank you. See you soon. Love you."

Her reply arrives immediately:
"Welcome back to the surface. We missed you."

I empty my glass.
I contemplate the books.
Now nothing's missing.

Epilogue

ELSIE

MATT

2:21 in the morning.

ELSIE

I took everything
I took it all downstairs.
Three bags of books.

MATT

Okay. How do you want to do this?

ELSIE

Your team will notice, won't they? That there's something at the
bottom of the hole. And they'll have to get it out. Then they'll know
it's me.

MATT

I've got gravel in my truck. We'll cover it all up: the bags, the books.
Nobody's going to figure it out. Tomorrow we'll fill it up and put
asphalt down. Tomorrow most of the work will be finished and my
team will be moving on to something else, another hole, another accident. It'll be our secret.

ELSIE
I move forward to the edge of the hole
ignoring the cones
the yellow DANGER tape
my fear of heights
and one by one I drop the bags into the hole
one bag of poetry and stories
one bag of novels
and one bag with all the copies of *Haven* I could find
all the copies with white covers
old editions
the new edition with the gold "Governor General's Award" sticker
the paperback edition
the translations.

I keep the copies on my desk
those inscribed by my mother:
To my dear Elsie. For everything.

MATT
I watch Elsie drop the bags into the hole one by one.
I think about the blown-up streets of Sarajevo
the ones in the photos I've seen in magazines
the ones in my visions, my nightmares.
I think about the message from Sanel Catic.
I think about the drawers, the bed, the apartment, all empty since my
ex left.
I think about what's left afterwards
and again I see my thumb which fits perfectly in the bullet holes of
Sarajevo.

Filling up the emptiness.
Filling in the absence.

I think about Alain and Nicole
my parents from here who wanted me
even when I was completely broken
when I didn't speak their language
when I was afraid of them
even when I tried to escape through the bathroom window.
I couldn't have done better.

From my pocket, I take out *Haven*
Gabrielle Sauriol's Sarajevo that will never be mine.

Hold on, Elsie. This one too.

MATT
ELSIE
And one more copy of *Haven*
one last little piece that floats on the surface.

ELSIE
My mother, finally coming to rest
settling down somewhere
like a bird that's reached its destination.

MATT
Here. Take a shovel.

ELSIE
MATT
Standing in the back of the pickup painted in the city's colours
sweat on our brows
our T-shirts soaked through
our arms getting eaten by mosquitoes
we shovel gravel on top of

the complete works of Gabrielle Sauriol
on top of
the writer Gabrielle Sauriol
on top of

ELSIE
my mother,
Gabrielle.

ELSIE
MATT
The books covered in gravel
disappear.

ELSIE
The more we empty gravel from the back of the pickup
the more my eyes fill up with water
at last.

ELSIE
MATT
The back of the pickup is empty
and the shovels are tied down inside the truck.

We collapse on the grass.
We look up at the stars.

ELSIE
She was never all mine
my mother.
Before she was gone all the time
she was always in her head

she hardly slept
she wrote parts of sentences on old envelopes
she talked to herself while she was making something to eat.

Maybe the most solid,
the most tangible mother I had
is the one made of paper that I just buried.

I'm crying
still
and Matej holds my hand,

MATT
Elsie's crying and I hold her hand without saying anything
because I feel like that's the right thing to do.

The sky is immense.
I think about Jasko and Zifa
disappeared
nestali
and about Elsie's mother
who'll always be here with her.
What's real and what we forget.

I blink
and it's no longer Elsie's hand in mine
it's no longer Elsie's skin touching mine
it's my mother's
I feel it in my veins.
For a very short moment
I remember my mother's voice
"Matej Matty Matty"

and my little fingers holding on to her brown hair.
I blink and everything disappears.

> *Silence, then we hear the sound of the surf. The waters of Discovery Passage.*

> *End.*

Acknowledgements

Mishka Lavigne would like to thank dramaturg Antoine Côté Legault for his insights, his calm, and his always pertinent questions. She would also like to thank playwright David Paquet, who accompanied the first and second draft of *Havre* at the Banff Centre for the Arts in 2015. I owe you both a debt of gratitude.

Thank you also to Patrizia Lombardi Acerra from the International Voices Project, who took a chance on this translation, and Jack Paterson and BoucheWHACKED! Theatre Collective for workshopping this work despite the challenges of the first few months of the COVID-19 pandemic.

Mishka Lavigne (she/her) is a playwright, screenwriter, and literary translator based in Ottawa/Gatineau. Her plays have been produced and developed in Canada, Switzerland, France, Germany, Australia, Haiti, and the United States. Her play *Havre* was awarded the 2019 Governor General's Literary Award for Drama (French). Her play *Copeaux*, a movement-based poetic creation piece with director Éric Perron, premiered in Ottawa in March 2020 and was also awarded the Governor General's Literary Award for Drama in 2021 as well as the Prix littéraire Jacques-Poirier. *Albumen*, her first play written in English, received the Prix Rideau Award for Outstanding New Creation in 2019 and the QWF Playwriting Prize in 2020. Mishka is currently working on a bilingual opera libretto with Montreal composer Tim Brady and on four new creations in French, as well as on some translation and screenwriting projects.

Neil Blackadder translates drama and prose from French and German. His translations of plays by Mishka Lavigne, Lukas Bärfuss, Ewald Palmetshofer, and Rebekka Kricheldorf have been produced in London, New York, Chicago, and elsewhere, and many others have been published and presented in staged readings. His translations of prose have appeared in journals including *Two Lines*, *Tupelo Quarterly*, and *Chelsea*. Other playwrights Neil has translated include Evelyne de la Chenelière, Ferdinand Schmalz, Thomas Arzt, and Maxi Obexer. Neil has been awarded grants by the National Endowment for the Arts, PEN, and the Howard Foundation, and held residencies at the Banff Centre and Art Omi.

First edition: March 2023
Printed and bound in Canada by Rapido Books, Montreal

Jacket art and design by Mélanie Simoneau
Author photo © Marianne Duval
Translator photo © Peter Bailley

PLAYWRIGHTS
CANADA PRESS

202-269 Richmond St. W.
Toronto, ON
M5V 1X1

416.703.0013
info@playwrightscanada.com
www.playwrightscanada.com
@playcanpress